2004 POE...

ONCE UPON A RHYME

IMAGINATION FOR A NEW GENERATION

Poems From Yorkshire & Lincolnshire

Edited by Jessica Woodbridge

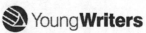 Young**Writers**

First published in Great Britain in 2005 by:
Young Writers
Remus House
Coltsfoot Drive
Peterborough
PE2 9JX
Telephone: 01733 890066
Website: www.youngwriters.co.uk

SB ISBN 1 84460 656 2

Foreword

Young Writers was established in 1991 and has been passionately devoted to the promotion of reading and writing in children and young adults ever since. The quest continues today. Young Writers remains as committed to engendering the fostering of burgeoning poetic and literary talent as ever.

This year's Young Writers competition has proven as vibrant and dynamic as ever and we are delighted to present a showcase of the best poetry from across the UK. Each poem has been carefully selected from a wealth of *Once Upon A Rhyme* entries before ultimately being published in this, our twelfth primary school poetry series.

Once again, we have been supremely impressed by the overall high quality of the entries we have received. The imagination, energy and creativity which has gone into each young writer's entry made choosing the best poems a challenging and often difficult but ultimately hugely rewarding task - the general high standard of the work submitted amply vindicating this opportunity to bring their poetry to a larger appreciative audience.

We sincerely hope you are pleased with our final selection and that you will enjoy *Once Upon A Rhyme Poems From Yorkshire & Lincolnshire* for many years to come.

Contents

George Pleasant   12
Saskia Lawson-Tovey (8)   13
Amelia Foote (8)   13
Freya Nicholson (7)   14

Kirkstall Valley Primary School, Leeds
Kane Francis (9)   14
Sophia Eades-Jones (9)   15
Safia Hagi (11)   15
Jack Priestley (10)   16
Lavinia Hill (10)   16
Molly Somerscales (9)   17
Amber Kaye-Kenyon (9)   17
Catherine Simpson (11)   18

Longroyde Junior School, Brighouse
Joseph D'Ambrogio (7)   18
Claycia Davis (9)   18
Jordan Moore (9)   19
Keyan Douglas (9)   19
Kelsey Gale (8)   19
Cassley Oliver (8)   20
Charlotte Probyn (8)   20
Ashley Kendall (7)   20
Kyle Binns (7)   21
Jake Adams (7)   21
Eden Sylvester (8)   21
Jordan Wigglesworth Torr (8)   22
Megan Smith (9)   22
Amy Birkby (8)   22
Paige Smith   23
Mary Ingle (8)   23
Amber Beever (8)   23
Andrew Ball   24
Gabrielle Smith (9)   24
Joe Javens (9)   24
Hannah Bishop-Crowther (7)   25
Nichol Coumont (7)   25
Emma Peace (9)   25
Georgina Thornton (9)   26
Sophie Parkin (9)   26

Charlotte Van Der Lijn (10)	54
Christopher Blessed (10)	54
Whitney Flounders (10)	55
Holly Cambridge (10)	56
Joel Mulholland (10)	56
Shellby McMahon (10)	57
Natalie Sinclair (10)	57
Andrew Lewis (10)	58
Natalie Moore (10)	58
Anne-Marie Roberts (10)	59
Jamie Mallender (10)	59
Hannah Wynne (10)	60
Keith Clarke (10)	60
Shara Burt (10)	61
Matthew Davies (10)	61
Tommy Stenton (10)	62
Brydie Raybould-Cridge (10)	62
Luke Wykes (11) & Jessica Melville (10)	63
Emily Thompson (10)	63
Joseph McGee (10)	64
Catrina Stanley (10)	64
Jordan Wykes (11)	65
Jamie Jones (10)	65
Gareth Thickett (10)	66
Felix Antons-Jones (10)	66
Dorothy Miles (11)	67
Louise Armstrong (10)	67
Harley White (10)	67
Charli Holland (10)	68
Carl Richardson (10)	68
Abigail Thompson (10)	69
Chrystal Bissenden (10)	69
Ryan McKenzie (10)	70

Stamford Junior School, Stamford

Sam Johnston (9)	70
Louis Grimoldby (10)	71
Michael Horrell (10)	71
Alison Murray (10)	72
Katie Noble (10)	72
Dan Wiggin (10)	73

Elizabeth Painter (10)	73
Thomas Pritchard (11)	74
Victoria Salt (10)	74
Edward Stout (11)	75
Sam Clulow (10)	75
Fred Forrest (10)	76
Rachel Richardson (10)	76
Oliver Anand (10)	77
Jack Lyons (10)	77
Kirsten O'Neill (10)	78
Amardeep Singh Bhaker (10)	79
Justin Bland (10)	80
Elinor Lloyd (10)	80
Angelina Radjenovic (10)	81
Emily Rowbotham (10)	81
Alice Reid (10)	82
Jamie Ridgeon (10)	83
James Wilde (11)	84
Izaac Grimoldby (10)	84
Chloë Powell (10)	85
Florence Thompson (10)	85
Josh Riddick (10)	86
Anna Roe (10)	86
Alexia Thorne (11)	87
Gabrielle Bangay (10)	87
Fleurie Crozier (10)	88
Chloe Stowers-Veitch (10)	88
Douglas Tawn (10)	89
Hebe Fox (10)	89
Victoria Burgess (10)	90
Guy Sinker (10)	90
Ella Grimoldby (10)	91
Alexander Griffin (10)	91
George Pears (10)	92
Catherine Terry (10)	92
Holly Archer (10)	93
Simon Taylor (10)	94
Nikki Bows (10)	95
Joe Cameron (10)	96

The Poems

Darkness

Darkness is black like ghosts flitting around.
It sounds like the film 'Wrong Turn',
It looks pitch-black like a churchyard at night,
It feels really scary,
It tastes really dry, like cornflakes with no milk,
It reminds me of walking around at night, listening
                              to creaky floorboards.

William Rudd (9)
Bicker Preparatory School, Boston

Fun!

Fun is yellow like a big yellow bouncy castle.
Fun sounds like laughter and screaming children.
Fun tastes like really fizzy sweets tickling your tongue.
Fun looks like a big bouncy castle full of children.
Fun smells like fizzy drinks, chocolate cakes and lots of sweets.
Fun reminds me of bouncing on a trampoline with my friend.

Bethany Barkway (9)
Bicker Preparatory School, Boston

Happiness

Happiness is blue like pear drops.
It reminds me of my friends coming to my house.
It feels like me yelling and my heart pumping,
It looks like a swimming pool with the wave machine going.
It sounds like giggling children and people telling jokes.

Zain Kirk (9)
Bicker Preparatory School, Boston

Laughter

Laughter is yellow like the sand at the beach.
It feels like my insides are queasy.
It sounds like happiness.
It smells like roller coasters at Skegness.
It tastes like ice cream, sweets and chocolate.
It looks like screaming and happiness.

Georgia Higgins (8)
Bicker Preparatory School, Boston

Happiness

Happiness is pink like candyfloss.
It reminds me of people screaming and shouting
on the biggest roller coaster in the park.
It smells like chewy sweets.
It tastes like melted chocolate.
It sounds like screaming laughter.
It feels like jumping about.

Katie Worrall (8)
Bicker Preparatory School, Boston

Fun

Fun is red - like the roller coaster at Skegness.
It tastes like candyfloss at the amusements.
It sounds like squealing, laughing.
It reminds me of the fair.
It looks like a slot machine for people aged eighteen and over.

Luke Grimer (8)
Bicker Preparatory School, Boston

Anger

I am angry.
I'm breathing heavily, my eyes are turning really red and hollow.
I'm starting to clench my fists.
I feel like I'm burning with anger,
I'm breathing anger.
I start to feel a growling from the inside of my heart.
Suddenly, a headache roars up from my brain;
As if I had been watching TV all week!
I've the sudden urge to go and tear out my insides and cry out.
Is it just me, or do I smell leaking fuel?
By now, my eyebrows are at a very steep angle, as I pull out my hand.
On my hand, I have a splodge of fuel,
My adrenaline is through the roof!
So I put my hand in my mouth and swallow.
I fly into the air and a ghostly spirit spurts out of me,
As I fall to the floor.
Relieved.

Peter Worrall (9)
Bicker Preparatory School, Boston

Laughter

Laughter is black like my friend's favourite colour. He is funny.
It tastes like a sherbet dip; which makes my mouth all fizzy
and tickles my mouth.
It feels like someone with a feather tickling me.
It smells like a newly baked loaf.
It reminds me of a very funny programme I watch.
It looks like not very much - just darkness - because
I close my eyes when I laugh.
It sounds like lots of things, because everyone has a different laugh.

William Campion (10)
Bicker Preparatory School, Boston

Hate

Hate is red like a blood pool.
It tastes like drinking diesel.
It sounds like a tree being chopped down
and being loaded onto a truck.
It looks like a devil.
It reminds me of an elephant charging towards you.
It feels like being choked by the neck.

Aaran Benjamin (10)
Bicker Preparatory School, Boston

Fear

Fear is black like a big black spider hanging from a web on my ceiling.
It feels like I am lost in a cave with lots of big scary bats flying about.
It reminds me of ghosts and witches coming to get me.
It tastes like I have just had a dry piece of toast
And my mouth is all dry.
It sounds like lots of loud and creepy noises like creaky floorboards.
It smells like a sofa that is burning and is on fire in my house.
It looks like a big, scary, hairy monster under my bed.

Lauren Stacey (10)
Bicker Preparatory School, Boston

Owl Poem

The owl, his eyes as dark as night
his feathers soft as a cushion
his claws grabbing mice, with a swoop.

Katie Kingswood (10)
Boston St Nicholas' CE Primary School, Boston

The Sea In Winter

The sea is as fierce as a grizzly bear
He crashes about like he does not care.
The choppy water flies against the sand
Causing destruction all over the land.

The wind is as evil as a devil's glare
Stirring around in the air
Grabbing things and throwing them around
Making a crashing, bashing sound.

The waves breaking and crunching on the rocks
Causing destruction on the docks
Like a giant munching and crunching on his lunch
Before the crabs get crunched
They swerve around finding their food
As we move.

Octavia Ross (10)
Boston St Nicholas' CE Primary School, Boston

Snakes Of The Sea

S wimming in the sea
N aked with me.
A s the coral reef clouds around me
K illing small fish
E xecution in its path
S wimming in the sea.

I n its own mind of his
N eeding something to eat.

S wimming in the sea
E legant in the swimming contest
A naconda in the sea.

Thomas Cox (10)
Boston St Nicholas' CE Primary School, Boston

Scorpion

The scorpion is a powerful creature
Its claws catch its food
Its tail poisons its enemies
Its skin is an armoured suit of metal
Its eyes are like it's just woken up
Its sandy desert home is a harsh place
A harsh creature for a harsh habitat.

The scorpion is a powerful creature
Its claws catch its food
The scorpion is like an armoured tank
Rolling through the desert.

Matthew Pennington (10)
Boston St Nicholas' CE Primary School, Boston

Monkey

The monkey is a funny man,
He swallows bananas as fast as he can.
Then he swings through the trees,
Through the wind, rain and breeze.

He's brown and furry, funny but brave,
He could even defeat a bear in a cave.
Then he would swing again from tree to tree,
Showing off in front of me.

He's like a funny circus clown,
Climbing up the branch and then back down.
Now he's tired, flat out,
Turn out the lights there's not a shout.

Jessica Pepperdine (10)
Boston St Nicholas' CE Primary School, Boston

Cat

It's an owl swooping to catch its prey
Watch it 'cause you never know
When it's going to pounce
It's loud with its voice
But quiet with its movements . . .
So watch out
First you think it's all nice and fluffy
Suddenly you look at its eyes
Those knives reflecting at you
Also it's the sea drowning a mouse with a bit of slobber
So watch out
It's quick
Miiii aaaa ooooo wwww!

Brontie Wallaard (9)
Boston St Nicholas' CE Primary School, Boston

Bump In The Night

When I am asleep in my bed
There's danger going around in my head.
Things going bump in the night
Giving me a terrible fright!
Howling noises through the wall,
A scary face on my ball!
Curtains blow and wind whistles,
Eyes staring as sharp as thistles!
Lights flicker on and off,
Flying around, a big fat moth!
A sickening sound coming from my door,
A creaking noise upon the floor!
I can't take this anymore,
A shouting voice as it said,
'Come on darling, you sleepyhead!'

Krystal Rodgers (10)
Great Coates Primary School, Grimsby

I Know Someone

I know someone who can click their shoulder.
I know someone who can get their thumb socket out.
I know someone who can flick their nostrils.
I know someone who can make their eyes go round and round.
I know someone who can do magic tricks.
I know someone who can stuff lots of popcorn in their mouth.
I know someone who can count backwards from 1,000.
I know someone who knows a boy who can do a back wheelie.
I know someone who can click their finger.
I know someone who can kick their behind
    And that person is me.

Amaan Hashmi-Ubhi (7)
Harewood CE Primary School, Leeds

I Know Someone

I know someone who can do the splits.
I know someone who can pull their leg to their tummy.
I know someone who can jump up high on a trampoline.
I know someone who can jump once on the table
    And that person is me.

Nyree Collict (8)
Harewood CE Primary School, Leeds

I Know Someone

I know someone who can go red in the face.
I know someone who can growl like a cat.
I know someone who can do a funny sound with her lips.
I know someone who can drink milk and it comes out of her nose.
I know someone who can sing like a man.
I know someone who can bark like a dog
    And that someone is me!

Rebekah Hooks (8)
Harewood CE Primary School, Leeds

I Know Someone

I know someone who can do their maths without talking.
I know someone who can eat vegetables all day long.
I know someone who can pop their own cheeks.
I know someone who can eat a piece of cake.
I know someone who can put their own leg up.
I know someone who can eat a bowl of chicken
    And that someone is me.

Seema Panesar (8)
Harewood CE Primary School, Leeds

I Know Someone

I know someone who can flare his nostrils in and out.
I know someone who can make a ruler float.
I know someone who can burp whenever he wants.
I know someone who can put his thumbs out of their sockets.
I know someone who can click his elbow.
I know someone who can bend his legs back so they touch his sides
    And that someone is me.

Joseph Williams (7)
Harewood CE Primary School, Leeds

I Know Someone

I know someone who can spin their tongue.
I know someone who can put 20 grapes in their ear.
I know someone who can balance on the world.
I know someone who can write fast.
I know someone who can eat fast.
I know someone who can run fast
    And that someone is me!

Kavita Panesar (8)
Harewood CE Primary School, Leeds

I Know Someone

I know someone who can twist their arm all the way round,
Without moving their hand.
I know someone who can take their thumbs out of their sockets.
I know someone who can do a 360 degree spin on their bike.
I know someone who eats sand and dirt.
I know someone who can see through walls.
I know someone who can balance a ruler on their straight hand
    And that someone is me!

Monica Rall (8)
Harewood CE Primary School, Leeds

I Know Someone

I know someone who can wiggle their eyebrows.
I know someone who can roll their eyes.
I know someone who can balance a ball under their nose.
I know someone who can pop their mouth.
I know someone who can click their finger.
I know someone who can skateboard really well.

Jordan Bury (7)
Harewood CE Primary School, Leeds

I Know Someone

I know someone who can do the splits.
I know someone who can balance a pencil under their nose.
I know someone who can click their shoulder.
I know someone who can lick their elbow.
I know someone who can bend their finger back.
I know someone who can go red.
I know someone who can balance a ruler on their nose.

Jasmine Nicholson (8)
Harewood CE Primary School, Leeds

I Know Someone

I know someone who can skip very fast,
I know someone who can do the splits,
I know someone who can do the cancan,
I know someone who can moo like a cow,
I know someone who can squeak like a mouse,
I know someone who can squeak like a monkey
    And that someone is me!

Georgina Trifunovic (8)
Harewood CE Primary School, Leeds

I Know Someone

I know someone who can flare their nostrils.
I know someone who can balance on their shoulders.
I know someone who can put their legs beside their body.
I know someone who can twist their arm right round.
I know someone who can do the splits right down.
I know someone who can put their legs round their neck
    And that someone is me!

Felicity Emmott (8)
Harewood CE Primary School, Leeds

I Know Someone

I know someone who can wiggle their ears.
I know someone who can sharpen a pencil until it is gone almost,
But has a little bit of lead left.
I know someone who can twist their arm without their hand moving.
I know someone who can burp when they want to.
I know someone who can do the splits very low on the floor.
I know someone who can scream the loudest
    And that's me!

Isabelle Garside (8)
Harewood CE Primary School, Leeds

I Know Someone

I know someone who can jump out of their bedroom window and land
on his trampoline.
I know someone who can make a ruler flat.
I know someone who can see through everything.
I know someone who can speak like Donald Duck.
I know someone who can eat sand.
I know someone who can put a snake up their nose
and make it come out of his mouth.
I know someone who can fire a bow and arrow with his legs and feet.

Thomas Hartley (8)
Harewood CE Primary School, Leeds

I Know Someone

I know someone who can spin their head.
I know someone who can talk like Donald Duck and Stitch.
I know someone who can do the splits for ten minutes.
I know someone who can click their shoulder.
I know someone who can put a pencil between their nose and mouth.
I know someone who can put their thumbs out of their sockets
    And that is me.

Lottie Hodson (7)
Harewood CE Primary School, Leeds

I Know Someone

I know someone who can do the splits.
I know someone who can lift the world.
I know someone who can read ten times faster than us
I know someone who can balance a grape on their nose.
I know someone who can go *pop* in their mouth.
I know someone who can balance a bucket on their nose
    And that person is me.

George Pleasant
Harewood CE Primary School, Leeds

I Know Someone

I know someone who can push their bones out of their sockets.
I know someone who can wiggle their ears without touching them.
I know someone who can do the splits right down.
I know someone who can bend their legs
so they are flat against their sides.
I know someone who can balance on one shoulder
without anything else touching anything.
I know someone who can click their shoulder.
I know someone who can speak like Donald Duck.
I know someone who can see through anything.
I know someone who can balance a ruler on their hand
without holding it.
    And that person is *me!*

Saskia Lawson-Tovey (8)
Harewood CE Primary School, Leeds

I Know Someone

I know someone who can make their thumbs come out
                                of their sockets.
I know someone who can twist their elbow round without
                                moving their hand.
I know someone who can balance on their shoulder.
I know someone who can flare their nose holes!
I know someone who can do the splits!
I know someone who can sing very, very, very well.
I know someone who can fold their legs in so they are
                                straight beside her.
I know someone who can see through everything.
I know someone who is rubbish at football.
I know someone who is very kind to people when they get hurt
    And that someone is me.

Amelia Foote (8)
Harewood CE Primary School, Leeds

I Know Someone

I know someone who can click her shoulder.
I know someone who can put her legs flat at her sides.
I know someone who can wrap her legs around her neck.
I know someone who can get her foot and touch her nose.
I know someone who can hold a pencil between her nose and mouth
  And that someone is me.

Freya Nicholson (7)
Harewood CE Primary School, Leeds

Classrooms Then And Now

Long wooden stick called the cane,
Get it on your hands . . . ooh, the pain!
Stuffed animals sitting at the table,
A hand is raised by a girl called Mabel.
There hangs a portrait of our beloved queen,
The best ruler of a land the world has ever seen.
Fidget-stoppers on your fingers, you're the one to blame,
Standing in front of the class, head hung in shame.
Children writing in their copy books,
Teacher turns, everyone gives funny looks.
In a Victorian school that's what would be seen,
You see someone get the cane . . . ooh, that teacher's mean!

Children sitting at their table wait till Miss comes in,
There's a piece of paper on the floor, quickly put it in the bin!
Kids not doing homework, what will Miss say?
She'll know it's missing, when she checks the homework tray.
At the question table it says, 'What is a lynx?'
There stands a boy called Kane, writing what he thinks.
In the different classrooms differing things you see,
I prefer nowadays. Then wasn't for me.

Kane Francis (9)
Kirkstall Valley Primary School, Leeds

Then And Now

Straight backs, silent rows, hands unseen.
Inspected by the teacher, shoes so clean.
Shiny pennies dropping into the patterned penny pot.
Silent children writing, trying not to blot.
All the desks in rows, never out of place.
A boy called Albert working, with a tired face.
In a classroom long ago these things you might see,
I wouldn't have liked to live then, it's just not me!

Backs bent over, chattering groups, the start of the day.
Register being called, there's always someone away.
Homework in the homework tray, someone's got it wrong.
He's got an excuse, 'We weren't given long.'
All the desks out of place,
Someone's pulling a funny face.
In Victorian times most kids were poor,
That's why I love living in 2004.

Sophia Eades-Jones (9)
Kirkstall Valley Primary School, Leeds

Playground

Hoops spinning, children whipping,
Jumping jacks dancing, children laughing,
Marbles rolling, people throwing,
Girls skipping, people singing.

Girls scoring, boys booing,
Girls skipping, girls singing,
Cards blowing, boys chasing,
Marbles banging, boys fighting.

These are the games in my playground.
Then was then and now is now.

Safia Hagi (11)
Kirkstall Valley Primary School, Leeds

Then You're A Lad From Leeds

If you can see the Victorian classroom of Armley Mills,
If you can see players celebrating at Elland Road
As Leeds United score a goal,
If you can see Kirkstall Valley Primary School,
Where children are playing happily,
If you can see Rhinos score a try,
Then you're a lad from Leeds.
If you can hear the whine of an aeroplane
Leaving Leeds/Bradford Airport,
If you can hear fireworks exploding over Kirkstall Abbey,
If you can hear the roar of the crowd
Shouting as Leeds United win,
Then you're a lad from Leeds.

Jack Priestley (10)
Kirkstall Valley Primary School, Leeds

Around The Classroom - Then And Now

Sums on the old squeaky blackboard,
Numeracy on a bright, shiny white board.

Dip pens scratching on the yellow copy books,
Gel pens rolling smoothly on the white, lined paper.

They look at the dull picture of Queen Victoria on the plain walls.
The children see their work on the bright and colourful display boards.

The pupils sit in rows with straight backs and hands unseen.
Children sit in groups with fiddling hands, sometimes chattering.

Children close their hands as they feel the object that's in them.
They carefully read the question and then write the answer.

Lavinia Hill (10)
Kirkstall Valley Primary School, Leeds

Classroom Life

Gertrude Elliot is my name.
Cup 'n' ball my favourite game!
I am here to tell you how it would be,
For a Victorian child in 1883!
They are really strict in these days you know,
But school is better than selling matches in the snow!
They give you the cane for almost everything you do,
So sometimes you're happy when you're poorly, or have the flu!
At the front of our large classroom stands
A picture of our beloved queen who rules lots of lands.
When we're writing with dip pens we're careful not to blot,
But it seems to get so smudged when you dip it in the pot.
White pinnies are what the girls wear,
But you have to be careful in case they tear.
My family isn't rich and my boss treats me like swine,
I wish I could live 100 years later, it's surely a better time.

Molly Somerscales (9)
Kirkstall Valley Primary School, Leeds

Leeds

If you can see the proud crouching lions outside the town hall,
If you can see an old and crumbly Kirktstall Abbey wall,
If you can see the bright amber and blue on match night, walking
                                        up Kirkstall Hill,
If you can see weaving machines banging to and fro at Armley at
                                        the mill,
Then you're a lass from Leeds.

If you can hear Hyde Park fireworks banging and zooming,
If you can hear the Rhino fans when they score a try shouting
                                        and booming,
If you can hear the water running down the River Aire,
If you can hear the cheer at Elland Road and wish that you were there,
Then you're a lass from Leeds.

Amber Kaye-Kenyon (9)
Kirkstall Valley Primary School, Leeds

A Girl's Pocket

Conkers she collected with her mum,
Bag of sweets, yummy yum.
Packet of chalk to draw on her top,
Peg doll girl called Mabel Mop.
Penny waiting to be handed over,
Ribbons from her hair and a four-leaf clover.

Pound coin to spend on sweets after school,
Swirly pencil to use and look cool.
Bobble to put her hair in a plait,
Yu-Gi-Oh! cards to swap and get back,
Teddy to play with, with her friends,
Ring she was told to remove before morning ends.

Catherine Simpson (11)
Kirkstall Valley Primary School, Leeds

Happiness

Happiness is blue like dancing in Heaven.
It sounds like the wind blowing in the air.
It tastes like delicious food on a plate.
It looks happy all around.
It feels soft like being wrapped in a blanket.

Joseph D'Ambrogio (7)
Longroyde Junior School, Brighouse

Silence

Silence sounds like when I stroke my fluffy slippers.
Silence reminds me of when I watch my beautiful fish swim
in the fish tank.
Silence is a really creamy colour, like silky ice cream.
Silence tastes like a melting bar of chocolate.
Silence feels like when I'm in a bath with loads of bubbles.
Silence looks like the clouds floating through the sky.

Claycia Davis (9)
Longroyde Junior School, Brighouse

Anger

Anger is red, like roses.
Anger is like my dog when he is mean.
Anger tastes like my mum's curry.
Anger feels like my hands on fire.
Anger is hard like the wall.
Anger looks like steam.
Anger is like a stick of rock.
Anger reminds me of hot chocolate.

Jordan Moore (9)
Longroyde Junior School, Brighouse

Love

Love reminds me of beautiful angels flying with white feathery wings.
Love is red like a rose and like cherry cheeks.
Love tastes like a juicy, watery strawberry on your tongue.
Love feels like my grandma's warm, cosy hug.
Love sounds like pink, kissable lips on your cheek.
Love looks like bright, colourful hearts.

Keyan Douglas (9)
Longroyde Junior School, Brighouse

Romance

Love is red like rosy cheeks.
It sounds like romantic dancing.
It tastes like hot chocolate.
It smells of lovely roses.
It looks like Heaven.
It feels like happiness.
It reminds me of when I fell in love.

Kelsey Gale (8)
Longroyde Junior School, Brighouse

Love

Love is red like roses.
It sounds like angels dancing.
It tastes like hot chocolate.
It smells of lovely roses.
It looks lovely inside.
It feels like a moment of glory.
It reminds me of when I fell in love.

Cassley Oliver (8)
Longroyde Junior School, Brighouse

Love

Love is pink like my lips.
It sounds like my heart pounding.
It tastes like love berries.
It smells like peach perfume.
It looks like a heart of love.
It feels like love at first sight.
It reminds me of kissing.

Charlotte Probyn (8)
Longroyde Junior School, Brighouse

Love

Love is pink like my lips.
It sounds like my heart pounding.
It tastes like strawberries.
It smells of warm chocolate.
It looks like pink and red petals flying in the breeze.
It feels like the world around you stops.
It reminds me of kissing.

Ashley Kendall (7)
Longroyde Junior School, Brighouse

Anger

Anger is red like a meteor.
It sounds like a big plane.
It tastes like a giant sweet.
It smells of a fire.
It looks evil.
It feels hot.

Kyle Binns (7)
Longroyde Junior School, Brighouse

Sadness

Sadness is blue like freezing cold water,
It sounds like thunder thumping,
It tastes like you're going to be sick.
It smells of smoke coming out of nowhere,
It looks like tears coming,
It feels like you'll never be happy again,
It reminds me of my best friend Eggzodia's head being burned.

Jake Adams (7)
Longroyde Junior School, Brighouse

Happiness

Happiness is yellow
like a spring flower.
It sounds like birds singing.
It tastes like sweet strawberries.
It smells of roses.
It looks like happiness and joy.
It feels soft.
It reminds me of flowers.

Eden Sylvester (8)
Longroyde Junior School, Brighouse

Silence

Silence tastes like sweets and red, flaming fireballs.
Silence feels like good behaved boys.
Silence reminds me of my friends, nice and helpful and kind people.
Silence looks like thin air in the sky with the birds and the clouds.
Silence is light red like the burning sun.
Silence sounds like kids being quiet and nobody talking.

Jordan Wigglesworth Torr (8)
Longroyde Junior School, Brighouse

Fun

Fun is a beaming yellow, like flowing custard, hot,
                              very sticky and gooey.
Fun sounds like a roaring river flowing down and down.
Fun tastes like a bowl of icing swirling round and round.
Fun feels like I am eating a big bar of Cadbury chocolate.
Fun reminds me when I went on holiday and I had a great time
                              at the water park.
Fun looks like a golden beam getting closer and closer.

Megan Smith (9)
Longroyde Junior School, Brighouse

Happiness

Happiness sounds like wine.
Happiness tastes like pizza.
Happiness feels like love.
Happiness reminds me of presents.
Happiness is pink.

Amy Birkby (8)
Longroyde Junior School, Brighouse

Fun

Fun is colourful yellow like boiling sun.
Fun sounds like exciting laughter and people exploring.
Fun would taste like millions of sweets with an exploding bun
and cakes.
Fun feels like swallowing chocolates.
Fun reminds me of seeing my cousins on Christmas Eve.
Fun looks like people having fun and giving lovely things to people.

Paige Smith
Longroyde Junior School, Brighouse

Love

Love feels like a burning heart that has been dropped in fire.
Love reminds me of a nice warm cuddle.
Love looks like trickling red blood.
Love is the colour of lava in a volcano.
Love sounds like an erupting volcano, ready to burst.
Love tastes like melting chocolate running down your throat.

Mary Ingle (8)
Longroyde Junior School, Brighouse

Fun

Fun feels like goodness and happiness.
Fun reminds me of exciting parties at Brewsters.
Fun looks like happiness and laughter.
Fun is an exciting blue like singing birds.
Fun sounds like laughter or happiness.
Fun tastes like a nice cold, cream chocolate sundae.

Amber Beever (8)
Longroyde Junior School, Brighouse

Silence

Silence is like quiet mice squeaking.
Silence is like the sparkling snow falling from the sky.
Silence is the colour of water.
Silence sounds like the clouds slowly moving in the sky.
Silence tastes like chocolate.
Silence feels like you're walking down the road with your mum.

Andrew Ball
Longroyde Junior School, Brighouse

Love

Love is red like a red rose.
It smells like fresh red apples.
It tastes like sweet potatoes.
It feels like soft cushions.
It sounds like gold, sprinkling water.
It reminds me of my first hug.

Gabrielle Smith (9)
Longroyde Junior School, Brighouse

Laughter

Laughter tastes like my grandma's hot dogs.
Laughter feels like me and my brother laughing.
Laughing sounds like a machine gun shooting.
Laughter looks like someone is happy and joyful.
Laughter reminds me of Christmas.
Laughter is orange like the sun floating down on me.

Joe Javens (9)
Longroyde Junior School, Brighouse

Love

Love is pink like flowers.
It sounds like birds in the air.
It tastes like the salty sea.
It smells of romantic tulips.
It looks like the natural world.
It feels like the hot desert.
It reminds me of red, red roses.

Hannah Bishop-Crowther (7)
Longroyde Junior School, Brighouse

Love

Love is pink like a sparkling diamond.
It sounds like a tinkling bell.
It tastes like my favourite chocolate.
It smells of baby powder.
It looks like a red heart.
It feels so good.
It reminds me of a beautiful sunny day.

Nichol Coumont (7)
Longroyde Junior School, Brighouse

Anger

It smells like gas and burnt metal.
It sounds like broken glass.
It feels like you've thrown glass.
It tastes like mushrooms.

Emma Peace (9)
Longroyde Junior School, Brighouse

Love

Love reminds me of two soft and snuggly
white doves flying in the sky.
Love is the colour of bright smooth pink,
like some really nice chunky lips.
Love tastes like a quiet, cosy kiss.
Love sounds like a fast, heavy waterfall
running through my heart.
Love looks like shining stars
glowing in the misty night sky.

Georgina Thornton (9)
Longroyde Junior School, Brighouse

Love

Love is red like roses.
Love is sweet like plums.
Love is soft like pillows.
Love reminds me of my mum.

Sophie Parkin (9)
Longroyde Junior School, Brighouse

Silence

Silence sounds like a grey feather
falling off a bird in the blue sky.
Silence looks like my beautiful fish
swimming in my tank.
Silence is a dull grey.
Silence tastes like gorgeous pasta.
Silence feels like my soft and comfy bed.

Jack Hamilton-Seaman (9)
Longroyde Junior School, Brighouse

Happiness

Happiness is like a red rose on the top of a cliff.
Happiness tastes like a white ice cream melting in my mouth.
Happiness feels like a beautiful blue sky.
Happiness sounds like a twittering bird whistling in the green trees.
Happiness looks like a beautiful, hot summer's day.

Elliott Hollingdrake (9)
Longroyde Junior School, Brighouse

Fear

Fear feels like whistling in the enormous green trees.
Fear sounds like a seagull going *'Erk, erk, erk!'*
Fear looks like a tiger eating a zebra.
Fear reminds me of when I get a smacked bum.
Fear tastes like a piece of fire in my mouth.

Harry Rawcliffe (9)
Longroyde Junior School, Brighouse

Happiness

Happiness is the lovely colours from the
happy bright rainbow in the beautiful blue sky.
Happiness tastes like lasagne.
Happiness feels like a cosy king-size bed and hairy blanket.
Happiness sounds like a bell at the end of a cool school day.
Happiness looks like the sun for the season of summer
and cosy clouds above the exciting turquoise sea.

Ilyas Afzal (9)
Longroyde Junior School, Brighouse

Happiness

Happiness sounds like birds singing in the trees.
Happiness is that day of fun on my bike.
Happiness is when I enjoy my new stuff.
Happiness is when I make new friends.
Happiness is being very excited on my birthday.
Happiness is when I got my new bedroom.

Saika Rahman (9)
Longroyde Junior School, Brighouse

Love

Love is crimson red like the blood flowing through my veins.
Love tastes like a chocolate biscuit.
Love feels like the hot sun on a summer's day.
Love sounds like a violin in a band.
Love looks like pretty fireworks going off in the midnight sky.
Love reminds me of my first girlfriend.

Cieran Huburn (9)
Longroyde Junior School, Brighouse

Love

Love is pink like a pink balloon.
It sounds like a bird singing and flying in the air.
It tastes like a sweet being eaten.
It smells of sugar and spice.
It looks like a love heart.
It feels like somebody getting married.
It reminds me of kissing.

Abigael Kemp (7)
Longroyde Junior School, Brighouse

Darkness

Darkness tastes like a big, dark, scary, muddy puddle.
Darkness feels like a massive spooky bat munching you up.
Darkness reminds me of an angry big mouse.
Darkness looks like black, dark air.
Darkness is scary, dull, black.
Darkness sounds like bats exploring in the night sky.

Oliver Stock (8)
Longroyde Junior School, Brighouse

Sadness

Sadness is light blue like a tear running down a cheek.
It sounds like water flowing down a hose pipe.
It tastes like a cold cup of tea.
It smells of dead flowers.
It looks like a gloomy face.
It feels like heavy rain.
It reminds me of Mummy being in hospital.

Aimee Mettrick (7)
Longroyde Junior School, Brighouse

Anger

Anger is red like the sun burning over you.
It sounds like screaming from a lobster boiling in the pan.
It tastes like fire in your mouth.
It smells of a red lobster cooking.
It looks like a burnt chicken.
It feels not very nice.
It reminds me of anger when I am cross.

Kieran Bennett (7)
Longroyde Junior School, Brighouse

Love

Love is pink like our lips.
It sounds like a bird singing in your head.
It tastes like a sweet being chewed.
It smells of the blue sky.
It looks like a piece of pink wrapping paper.
It feels beautiful and very warm.
It reminds me of some of my friends.

Cerys Newton (7)
Longroyde Junior School, Brighouse

Fun

Fun feels like I'm having a really good time with my friends.
Fun is like the lovely light blue sky.
Fun sounds like everyone having a good time.
Fun tastes like I'm having a Galaxy chocolate bar.
Fun makes me feel really nice.
Fun reminds me of Aaron playing with me.

Jordan Spencer (8)
Longroyde Junior School, Brighouse

Fun

Fun looks like I am having a really happy, fun time.
Fun is like a beautiful blue sky.
Fun sounds like people having a good time.
Fun tastes like having fun.
Fun feels like a shiny sports car.
Fun reminds me of a good time.

Dylan Williamson (8)
Longroyde Junior School, Brighouse

Fun

Fun looks like the shining yellow, hot sun.
Fun is bright blue like the bright blue sea.
Fun sounds like the breeze and the rustling green leaves on the trees.
Fun tastes like a creamy Galaxy chocolate bar.
Fun feels like playing on the red swings and turquoise slide.
Fun reminds me of playing with my funny fun friends.

Arfa Ahmed (8)
Longroyde Junior School, Brighouse

Fun

Fun feels like a bouncing ball.
Fun reminds me of chocolate.
Fun looks like a bottle of water.
Fun is a shining silver smile.
Fun sounds like a whistle blowing.
Fun tastes like a juicy apple.

Calum Menzies (8)
Longroyde Junior School, Brighouse

Laughter

Laughter is like the colour of a blue elephant.
Laughter sounds like a man who needs the toilet.
Laughter smells like someone's just come off the toilet.
Laughter looks like a clown who has just got wet.
Laughter tastes like you have just eaten a joke book.
Laughter reminds me of when my friends told me a funny joke.

Theo Senior (9)
Longroyde Junior School, Brighouse

Happiness

Happiness is yellow like the sun in the sky.
Happiness sounds like bells in a church.
Happiness smells like red roses.
Happiness looks like a twinkling star.
Happiness feels like hugging your mum.
Happiness tastes like a bag of sweets.
Happiness reminds me of when my brother was born.

Adam Middleton (9)
Longroyde Junior School, Brighouse

Love

Love is the colour red when you get a Valentine.
Love sounds like people kissing.
Love smells like a big dinner cooking.
Love looks like you when you see someone you like.
Love feels like when someone asks you out.
Love tastes like chocolates.
Love reminds me of my family.

Jade Hawkins (9)
Longroyde Junior School, Brighouse

Love

Love is gold like a star in the sky.
It smells like strawberry pies.
It tastes like hot chocolate.
It feels like fluffy fur.
It reminds me of hugging my mum.

Jack Roberts (9)
Longroyde Junior School, Brighouse

Fun

Fun is bright yellow and shines like the sun.
Fun sounds like a merry-go-round song constantly repeating.
Fun smells like freshly-baked cookies with double chocolate.
Fun looks like a TV star singing your favourite song.
Fun feels like riding a dolphin across the sea.
Fun tastes like excitement crackling in your mouth.
Fun reminds me of Christmas, opening all my presents.

Carys Rewhorn (9)
Longroyde Junior School, Brighouse

Fear

Fear is like a black bull charging towards you.
Fear sounds like a snake hissing to strike.
Fear smells like a dark creature letting out some gas.
Fear looks like a haunted demon watching every step you take.
Fear feels like a dark shadow stabbing with every move.
Fear tastes like eating a pig's brain.
Fear reminds me of getting into big, *big trouble.*

Martin Dawson (9)
Longroyde Junior School, Brighouse

Fun

Fun is the colour of the bright stars shining gold.
Fun sounds like a choir singing.
Fun smells like an apple pie.
Fun looks like a king and queen's crown.
Fun feels like having a good time in a club.
Fun tastes like a chocolate world.
Fun reminds you of seeing your best friend.

Jazmin Simpson-Taylor (9)
Longroyde Junior School, Brighouse

Fun Poem

Fun is good like a green-golden fish.
Fun is good when you need to wash a dish.
Fun is good like my Sugar Puff with lots of honey on it.
Fun is good when Chris Benoit gets pinned.
Fun is good when you wash your face with cold water.
Fun is good when you have a nice hot pizza.
Fun is good when I get reminded of Xbox.

Feroz Khan (9)
Longroyde Junior School, Brighouse

Happiness

Happiness is pink like a cute little pig.
Happiness sounds like laughing.
Happiness smells like hot chocolate on a Sunday night.
Happiness looks like my friend's face.
Happiness feels like eating a chocolate bar.
Happiness reminds me of my family's party.

Bethany Hamilton (9)
Longroyde Junior School, Brighouse

Sadness

Sadness is blue when getting hurt.
Sadness sounds like an eagle screeching.
Sadness smells like a raw egg.
Sadness looks like a waterfall just dropped.
Sadness feels like being thrown on ice.
Sadness tastes like an onion.
Sadness reminds me of an old friend who hurt me.

Matthew Schofield (9)
Longroyde Junior School, Brighouse

Love

Love is like a big red rose.
Love sounds like your heart drumming inside.
Love smells like a big strawberry ice cream.
Love looks like a big red rose.
Love is a really good feeling that's ready to burst out.
Love tastes like a strawberry cake.
Love reminds me of a really big flower with red petals.

Nathan Canavan (9)
Longroyde Junior School, Brighouse

Fun

Fun is pink like candyfloss at a fairground.
Fun sounds like my mum when I tidied my room.
Fun smells like a gigantic tub of melted chocolate.
Fun looks like a key to a palace.
Fun feels like a guinea pig's fur.
Fun tastes like a massive bag of sweets.
Fun reminds me of Christmas Day.

Jenny Schofield (9)
Longroyde Junior School, Brighouse

Fun

Fun is red like a hot cup of tea.
Fun is the sound of the feeling in me.
Fun smells like fresh air by the sea.
Fun looks like you and me.
Fun feels great, deep inside.
Fun tastes fun, free and wild.
Fun reminds me of *my life!*

Emma Long (9)
Longroyde Junior School, Brighouse

Fun

Fun is blue like a party getting started.
Fun sounds like excited children playing and shouting.
Fun smells like party food.
Fun looks like playful children.
Fun feels like me at a party.
Fun tastes like a chocolate bar.
Fun reminds me of watching my best TV film.

Mackenzie Bennett (9)
Longroyde Junior School, Brighouse

Anger

Anger is as red as a devil.
Anger sounds like someone screaming when they have done
something wrong.
Anger smells like someone who has pooped in someone's face.
Anger looks like my sister when I have done something wrong.
Anger feels like me getting a smack on the bum.
Anger tastes like you have just eaten a sour sweet.
Anger reminds me of the time when I fell off my bike.

Jessica Cording (9)
Longroyde Junior School, Brighouse

Love

Love is red like a heart.
Love sounds like the birds tweeting.
Love smells like new perfume.
Love looks like flowers blossoming.
Love feels like excitement.
Love tastes like Dairy Milk chocolate.
Love reminds me of when I went to Florida.

Robyn Sykes (9)
Longroyde Junior School, Brighouse

Happiness

Happiness is red like a rose.
Happiness sounds like a twinkle of toes.
Happiness smells like fresh air from the sky.
Happiness looks like a twinkle in a star.
Happiness feels like love that will never die.
Happiness tastes like Dairy Milk chocolate.
Happiness feels like love at first sight.

William Tolley (9)
Longroyde Junior School, Brighouse

Fun

Fun is like the colour yellow.
Fun sounds like when you are laughing.
Fun smells like a McDonald's ready to be eaten.
Fun looks like when you are screaming on a really good roller coaster.
Fun feels like when you have just won a prize at the circus.
Fun tastes like a KFC.
Fun reminds me of the time I spent with my mum and dad
                                    at Wacky Warehouse.

Javene Robinson (9)
Longroyde Junior School, Brighouse

Happiness

Happiness sounds like a dolphin throwing itself in the smooth sea.
Happiness is bright yellow like the hot-flamed sun shining bright.
Happiness reminds me of the warm sea that is gleaming in the
                                    boiling sun.
Happiness is orange like the brightest Hallowe'en lantern.
Happiness tastes like sweets that taste the best.
Happiness feels like a brand new day starting.

Marinthe De Bokx (9)
Longroyde Junior School, Brighouse

Love

Love is like soft roses flying away in the breeze.
Love sounds like people kissing.
Love smells like waking up to a bright sunny morning.
Love looks like my baby sister's face smiling at me.
Love tastes like a sweet, sweet.
Love reminds me of clouds looking like hearts in the sky, floating away.

Xenia Kaur Ardawa (9)
Longroyde Junior School, Brighouse

I Wish . . .

I wish the world was chocolate cake,
I wish I lived by a big blue lake.
I wish I was rich and cool,
I wish I had a swimming pool.
I wish I could play away,
Instead of going to school all day.

I wish I had a million pounds,
I wish I had some barking hounds,
I wish I was a dancing queen,
I wish that people were not mean.
I wish I was a superstar,
Driving around in a fancy car.

I wish I was gorgeous looking,
I wish I was better than Gordon Ramsey at cooking.
I wish I had an Olympic gold,
I wish I never had to be old.
I wish that I was never ill,
That everything was free and had no bill.

If all my wishes did come true,
The world would be as good as new!

Chloe Hoult (8)
Longroyde Junior School, Brighouse

Fun

Fun is like when you have won an amazing race
and you can taste the victory.
Fun feels like me getting something I've always wanted,
like an electric scooter.
Fun sounds like you are at a circus
and when a clown makes you laugh.
Fun looks like a rushing giant wave splashing towards you.
Fun reminds me of when we had a disco.
Fun is like watching the clouds rushing past you.

Joshua Coldwell (9)
Longroyde Junior School, Brighouse

Darkness

Darkness sounds spooky, with a ghost coming towards you,
shaking you with thunder and lightning.
Darkness tastes like a hurricane, making you go round and round,
making you get sick.
Darkness feels gloomy like when you can't see
and a car comes out of the dark and runs you over flat.
Darkness reminds me of when somebody ran my foot over,
and how I felt while I was crying.
Darkness looks like you're not doing anything when you're bored.
Darkness is pitch-black like a night when a wolf is howling.

Jessica Bostock (8)
Longroyde Junior School, Brighouse

Anger

Anger tastes like eating a spicy curry.
Anger feels like hitting someone like a boxing bag.
Anger sounds like a piano hitting the floor.
Anger is red like a jar of blood.

Callum Murrell (9)
Longroyde Junior School, Brighouse

Darkness

Darkness is like a sloppy, slimy, snotty grey.
It tastes like the wind floating along the darkness.
It feels like the moon is shining right in front of me.
It sounds like the shadowy darkness is singing and whistling
through my fingers.
It looks like yucky, slimy, runny snot.
It reminds me of a nasty, horrible, slimy film I watched.

Daniel Simpson (9)
Longroyde Junior School, Brighouse

Fun

Fun is bright like blue and pink.
Fun sounds like a party link.
Fun smells like a big red rose.
Fun looks like children with bows.
Fun feels like the sun's here for weeks.
Fun tastes like a bag full of sweets.

Hayley Thompson (10)
Longroyde Junior School, Brighouse

Love

Love is red like Longroyde's school jumper.
Love sounds like an angel on a harp.
Love smells like my new perfume.
Love looks like my happy face.
Love feels like my mum giving me a hug.
Love tastes like a big chunk of chocolate.
At last love reminds me of my mum and dad.

Kirsten Swain (9)
Longroyde Junior School, Brighouse

Laughter

Laughter is green like a cat dancing.
Laughter sounds like a monkey saying, *'Ooh ah ea!'*
Laughter smells like curry on lovely brown rice.
Laughter looks like the perfect summer flowers.
Laughter feels like someone's just kicked someone on the bottom.
Laughter tastes like really nice chocolate.
Laughter reminds me of the other day when my friends kept on
slapping me.

Qasim Akhtar (9)
Longroyde Junior School, Brighouse

Darkness

Darkness is black and bold like in the night.
Darkness is quiet and sightless and frightless.
Darkness smells dirty and fluffy.
Darkness is bad, upsetting and mad.
Darkness feels heavy and cold.
Darkness tastes like dry food.
Darkness reminds me of my mum's mad eyes.

Corey Gayle (10)
Longroyde Junior School, Brighouse

Happiness

Happiness is the colour of pink,
It tastes like crispy Yorkshire puddings being demolished
by my mouth,
It smells like my mum's cooking when she's making Mexican wraps,
It looks like tiny babies bursting into laughter,
It sounds like peaceful music flowing through my ears,
It feels like a tall necked giraffe licking my hand for food.

Hannah Wood (8)
Misson Primary School, Doncaster

Happiness

Happiness is the colour of bright blue,
It tastes like warm spaghetti steaming on a plate,
It smells like fresh blossom bursting out of their buds,
It looks like the sunlight as bright as it could ever be,
It sounds like the refreshing songs of the birds singing in the trees,
It feels like the softness of warm fluff.

Dugald Fraser (8)
Misson Primary School, Doncaster

Happiness

Happiness is the colour of yellow,
It tastes like spaghetti bolognese ready to eat,
It smells like roses fresh from the ground,
It looks like Euro Disney castle high up in the sky,
It sounds like the Black Eyed Peas singing as loud as they can,
It feels like the sunshine steaming hot on my back.

Thomas Constantine (7)
Misson Primary School, Doncaster

Happiness

Happiness is the colour of cold blue,
It tastes like strawberries and ice cream melting on my tongue,
It smells like pizza sizzling in a hot oven,
It looks like a hedgerow of flowers blooming in the scorching sun,
It sounds like birds singing in a still oak tree,
It feels like a cool breeze running across my skin.

Jacob Pavlou (8)
Misson Primary School, Doncaster

Happiness

Happiness is the colour of light green,
It tastes like cold yummy salad with water sprinkled over the top,
It smells like soft marshmallows melting on the BBQ,
It looks like people smiling,
It sounds like people laughing,
It feels like people are being nice to you.

Jake Soper (9)
Misson Primary School, Doncaster

Happiness

Happiness is the colour of blue,
It tastes like my grandma's Yorkshire pudding and gravy,
It smells like salt and vinegar crisps,
It looks like my fish in the pond rushing around like bubble cars,
It sounds like people tapping a little tune on the table,
It feels like you're flying in the air with all kinds of birds.

Jenny Jackson (8)
Misson Primary School, Doncaster

Happiness

Happiness is the colour red,
It tastes like a bag of blazing hot, salty chips,
It smells like steaming hot lasagne, pleasant and bright,
It looks like a dragster, sleek and powerful,
It sounds like the engine, well made but deafening,
It feels like my cat, soft and purring.

Jack Constantine (9)
Misson Primary School, Doncaster

Happiness

Happiness is the colour of pink,
It tastes like cucumber so juicy and soft,
It smells like pink roses in the house in a vase,
It looks like my sister laughing and giggling,
It sounds like my mum washing up,
It feels like my covers soft and cosy.

Megan Kershaw (7)
Misson Primary School, Doncaster

Happiness

Happiness is the colour of green,
It tastes like ice cream dripping down my tongue,
It smells like toast roasting on the fire,
It looks like my presents that keep coming in different shapes,
It sounds like church bells ringing in the wind,
It feels like a relaxing hot bath.

Aron Thompson (8)
Misson Primary School, Doncaster

Happiness

Happiness is the colour of red,
It tastes like hot brown chips with ketchup,
It smells like lovely home-made soup with bread,
It looks like children playing in the playground,
It sounds like birds singing in the tree,
It feels like a small squeaky guinea pig.

Joshua Slack (7)
Misson Primary School, Doncaster

Happiness

Happiness is the colour of shiny gold,
It tastes like cooked spaghetti bolognese,
It smells like a new morning,
It looks like a fast shiny motorbike,
It sounds like Big Ben's chiming,
It feels like a lovely hot bath.

Reece Burbage (8)
Misson Primary School, Doncaster

Happiness

Happiness is the colour of yellow,
It tastes like raspberry ripple ice cream melting on my tongue,
It smells like flowers fresh from the garden,
It looks like children playing happily in the playground,
It sounds like children laughing in the playground,
It feels like a dog's furry coat.

Harry Taylor (7)
Misson Primary School, Doncaster

Happiness

Happiness is the colour of blue,
It smells like roast duck just come from the China Rose,
It tastes like a Sunday lunch straight from the oven,
It looks like snow just sat on a frozen pond,
It sounds like party poppers popping at a party,
It feels like a gorgeous apple just come from the grocers.

Ian Love (8)
Misson Primary School, Doncaster

Happiness

Happiness is the colour of blue,
It tastes like chocolate shortcake, double chocolate and yummy,
It smells like my little puppy when he has a bubble bath,
It looks like my birthday presents, all different shapes and sizes,
It sounds like church bells all rusty, brown and old,
It feels like water slithering through my fingers.

Jack Wells (8)
Misson Primary School, Doncaster

Happiness

Happiness is the colour of bright red,
It tastes like chestnuts from the fire,
It smells like roses that have just burst into bloom,
It looks like children playing happily in the playground,
It sounds like people crying for joy,
It feels like riding on a horse with the wind blowing on your face.

Beth Sutcliffe (8)
Misson Primary School, Doncaster

Happiness

Happiness is the colour of gold,
It tastes like marshmallows roasted on a fire,
It smells like colourful flowers swaying in a gentle breeze,
It looks like crazy chickens clucking and hopping around,
It sounds like cheerleaders performing at a national competition,
It feels like a roller coaster tipping upside down!

Robynne Tweedale (8)
Misson Primary School, Doncaster

Happiness

Happiness is the colour of bright yellow,
It tastes like chocolate melting in my mouth,
It smells like bacon sizzling in a pan,
It looks like a field of flowers all bright and multi-coloured,
It sounds like birds singing in the breeze,
It feels like a silk scarf all smooth and light.

Jack Cawkwell (7)
Misson Primary School, Doncaster

Happiness

Happiness is the colour of red,
It tastes like strawberries fresh from the field,
It smells like flowers straight from the garden,
It looks like a meadow full of butterflies,
It sounds like soft music flowing through my ears,
It feels like cotton wool touching my hand.

Melissa Lingard (8)
Misson Primary School, Doncaster

Happiness

Happiness is the colour purple,
It tastes like popcorn crunching in my mouth,
It smells like pancakes sizzling in the pan,
It looks like flowers swaying in the breeze,
It sounds like horses neighing in the field,
It feels like my bed all soft and cuddly.

Melissa Anderson (7)
Misson Primary School, Doncaster

Happiness

Happiness is the colour of pink,
It tastes like chips with salt and vinegar on,
It smells like cheese and onion crisps just about to be eaten!
It looks like somebody smiling at you and me,
It sounds like cheerful music or a playing band,
It feels like rabbit fur running through your fingers.

Kelsey Glasson (7)
Misson Primary School, Doncaster

Happiness

Happiness is the colour of violet,
It tastes like sherbet fizzing on my tongue,
It smells like perfume all sweet scented,
It looks like playful puppies all cute and cuddly,
It sounds like a kitten softly purring,
It feels like fur all fluffy and snugly.

Alicia Jackson (7)
Misson Primary School, Doncaster

The Prayer Of The Snake

Dear Lord,
Lord I do not ask a lot of You,
only that I wish I had legs
and I didn't have to slither and slide.
Oh Lord please don't let my skin rip anymore.
Please make delicious food mine . . .
like chicken, I long for food . . .
mmm.
Amen.

Jordan Harvey (11)
Mount St Mary's RC Primary School, Leeds

The Prayer Of The Bear

Dear God

Why when people see me do they run away in fear?
Also why do I have to hide away deep in the forest, away from people?
Nobody comes to visit me.
Lord why did You make me the way I am?
I like to see people.
I ask again Lord why do people run away from me?
And when I walk past trees why in terror do the birds fly out?
I see signs with pictures of me on them and they say *warning!*
Why did You give me a cloak of black fur?
  O Lord,
        All I want is to be normal.
                        Amen.

Danny Chappelow (11)
Mount St Mary's RC Primary School, Leeds

The Prayer Of The Bear

O Lord
why don't You help me?
Locked up in a crammed cage.
Helpless.
Why did You make me the way I am?
I am so big and clumsy,
why didn't You make me small?
Why didn't You give me wings
so I could fly freely in the sky?
Instead I have to crawl along the horrible floor.
Why do I have dark fur?
Couldn't I have bright colours like a butterfly?
Please God help me!
Get me out of this horrible place.
Please!

Zoe Landale (11)
Mount St Mary's RC Primary School, Leeds

The Prayer Of The Baby Seal

Dear God,
    Please help me!
I am not like the others,
    Why punish me?
I am the lonely one,
    I think it is because I am the youngest,
People laugh at me. *Why?*
    What have I done?
I have grey, silky skin. Why me?
    Couldn't I have had colourful skin like butterflies,
Instead of slithery and wet?
    I do like my whiskers though, they tickle,
I have something to say:
    Take me *away.*
Amen.

Hailey McVeigh (10)
Mount St Mary's RC Primary School, Leeds

The Prayer Of The Lion

Dear God,

Why do You let them trap me in a cage?
Why did You give me long fur around my face?
People throw me meat.
They stare, glare and laugh at me.
I live in boredom.
I feel abandoned.
Why did You give me a heavy coat of fur?
Why can't I be free to run wild and do my own thing?
O Lord, please set me free and make my dream come true.

Chelsie Stanley (11)
Mount St Mary's RC Primary School, Leeds

Prayer Of The Goldfish

Dear Lord,

I'm free at last in the pond!
No longer trapped in the prison.
Thank You!

I have friends, funny friends.
I meet them whenever I want to.
I play with them whenever I want to.

The pond you fill with delicious plants
So Deeeelicious . . . mmm
Where was I?
Oh! Thank You for my tail and fins,
The eyes that can see,
The clean water,
And the scales that are the colour of golden sand.

Thank You
            Amen.

Puja Patel (11)
Mount St Mary's RC Primary School, Leeds

The Prayer Of The Fox

Dear God
Why do You make us food for dogs?
Is it that you don't like us?
Are we drag toys for men and their horses?
Or just targets for people to shoot at?
But I do love my orange colour and white tail.
So please save us from those devils!

Samuel Crabbe (11)
Mount St Mary's RC Primary School, Leeds

What Is This?

What is thunder?
God laying a golden egg.
Why does it rain?
Because God's on the loo.
What are hailstones?
On a cold day, rain falls down
It falls so fast it freezes to ice.
What is a rainbow?
God mixing painting colours together.
What is lightning?
The sun falling apart.

Liam Cumbor (11)
Sandringham Primary School, Doncaster

Fun Draw

Fun
Draw
Found my shoe
Seesaw
Knock on the door
Fine
Pen
A big fat hen
Sticks
Fix
We're all in a fix
Nee
Naw
Fell on the floor.

Daniel Edwards (10)
Sandringham Primary School, Doncaster

Weather Questions

What is thunder?
Thunder is when God gets angry and he growls.
Why does it rain?
It rains because God cries.
What are hailstones?
Hailstones are when God holds a bag of frozen peas and empties it.
Where does the wind go?
The wind goes to the people who are cold and there is only hot.
What is fog?
Fog is smoke coming from the sky.

Jessica Barber (10)
Sandringham Primary School, Doncaster

My Mum: Angel Face

'Mummy why are you honest?'
'Because the angels blessed me.'
'Mummy why are you so pretty?'
'Because I have the face of an angel.'
'Mummy why does my heart beat?'
'Because it's an angels' harp singing its music.'
'Mummy why can't I be honest?'
'You are, you just don't notice.'
'Mummy why can't I be pretty?'
'You are, don't think you aren't,
Because you're like my twin sister
You just don't notice.'

Nadine Lafayette (10)
Sandringham Primary School, Doncaster

What Is?

What is an ear?
A secret listening device.
What is a nose?
A freezer that carries mushy peas in.
What is a mouth?
A chatterbox that never stops.
What are eyes?
Two pickled onions gone mouldy.

Charlotte Van Der Lijn (10)
Sandringham Primary School, Doncaster

Kung Fu

Kung
Fu
I ran to the zoo
Me
Draw
The tigers went roar
Live
Licks
The birds were holding sticks
Heaven's
Gate
The lions ate
Pine
Hen
The monkeys stayed in their den.

Christopher Blessed (10)
Sandringham Primary School, Doncaster

Kung Fu

Kung
Fu
I hopped to the zoo.
Sea
Door
The lion scraped his claw.
Hive
Bricks
The panda chewed sticks.
Heaven
Gate
The elephants ate.
Fine
Pen
The cubs' den.
Devon
Delve
The zookeepers shelve.
Dirt clean
Fort clean
The monkeys were the best thing
I've ever seen.
Myth team.
Fix team
The alligators were dark green.
Heaven mean
Late mean
The giraffe is lean.
Pine bean.
Kenty
Now it's time to go with my dog
Renty.

Whitney Flounders (10)
Sandringham Primary School, Doncaster

Bomb Brew

Bomb
Brew
I went to Peru.
Sea
Shore
I walked through the door.
Live
Dish
I saw a fish.
Heaven
Skate
I must see the swordfish before I'm late.
Sign
Hen
A secret den.

Holly Cambridge (10)
Sandringham Primary School, Doncaster

What Is?

What is Earth?
A giant gobstopper.
What is a river?
A giant cup of water.
What is a mountain?
A freezing cold ice lolly.
What is grass?
The Earth's hair.

Joel Mulholland (10)
Sandringham Primary School, Doncaster

Kung Fu

Kung
Fu
I hopped to the zoo.
Sea
Door
The lion scraped his claw.
Hive
Bricks
The panda chewed sticks.
Heaven
Gate
The elephants ate.
Fine
Pen
The cubs' den.

Shellby McMahon (10)
Sandringham Primary School, Doncaster

What Is?

What is green?
A pile of grass.
What is red?
A field of poppies.
What is gold?
A shiny star twinkling in the sky.
What is black?
Midnight.

Natalie Sinclair (10)
Sandringham Primary School, Doncaster

Fun Drew

Fun
Drew
I went to the zoo.
Sea
Shore
Lions go roar.
Alive
Twix
The monkey was in a fix.
Bedding
Cake
The bear fell in the lake.

Andrew Lewis (10)
Sandringham Primary School, Doncaster

What Is?

What is green?
A pile of grass.
What is red?
A field of poppies.
What is gold?
A shiny star
Twinkling in the sky.
What is black?
Midnight.

Natalie Moore (10)
Sandringham Primary School, Doncaster

Hong Do

Hong
Do
I hopped to the zoo.
Knee
Gnaw
I saw a boar.
Jive
Sticks
I saw a tiger eating toothpicks.
Devon
Plate
It was getting late.
Hive
Den
I went home again.

Anne-Marie Roberts (10)
Sandringham Primary School, Doncaster

What Is?

What is mashed potato?
A bowl of cotton wool.
What is an orange?
A bouncy ball.
What is a chocolate?
A brown brick.
What is candyfloss?
Pink snow on a stick.

Jamie Mallender (10)
Sandringham Primary School, Doncaster

Kong Fu

Kong
Fu
I legged it to the zoo.
See
Saw
It lasted for evermore.
Live
Twix
The squirrel collected some sticks.
Bedding
Cake
The lion ate some steak.
Pine
Pen
The hen went in the den.

Hannah Wynne (10)
Sandringham Primary School, Doncaster

What Is?

What are planets?
Nine bouncy balls.
What is Mars?
A bright red fireball.
What is Saturn?
A round head with
Different coloured ribbons around it.
What is the sun?
A great big beach ball in the sky.

Keith Clarke (10)
Sandringham Primary School, Doncaster

Kung Fu

Kung
Fu
The fish are in the zoo.
See
Saw
The fish are getting sore.
My
Sticks
They're all in a fix.
Heaven
Mate
They're going to be bait.
Sign
Hen
They have all gone with them.

Shara Burt (10)
Sandringham Primary School, Doncaster

What Is?

What is a toilet?
It is a flooded bowl.
What is a sink?
It is a small waterfall.
What is a bath tub?
It is a miniature ocean.
What is a shower?
It is a huge hosepipe.

Matthew Davies (10)
Sandringham Primary School, Doncaster

Fun Drew

Fun
Drew
I went to the zoo
Sea
Shore
Lions go roar
Alive
Twix
The monkey was in a fix
Bedding
Cake
The bear fell in the lake
Pine
Pen
The hen ran into the pen.

Tommy Stenton (10)
Sandringham Primary School, Doncaster

What Is?

What is a carrot?
An orange rocket about to set off.
What is a biscuit?
A giant's crumb fallen from the sky.
What are peas?
Rabbit droppings on your plate.
What's a pineapple?
A porcupine in the grass.

Brydie Raybould-Cridge (10)
Sandringham Primary School, Doncaster

Boo Hoo

Boo
Hoo
I zoomed to the zoo
Key
Door
The lions ruined the floor
Live
Sticks
The monkeys ate a Twix
Heaven
Gate
The donkey said, 'Hello mate!'
Blind
Hen
The hen went into the pen.

Luke Wykes (11) & Jessica Melville (10)
Sandringham Primary School, Doncaster

What Is?

What is spaghetti?
A plate full of worms.

What is an egg?
A giant's eyeball.

What is an orange?
A cockerel's bum.

What is a biscuit?
A mouse's 4X4 wheel.

Emily Thompson (10)
Sandringham Primary School, Doncaster

Fun Drew

Fun
Drew
I pegged it to the zoo
See
More
It's a great, wild boar
Live
Mix
The monkeys throw sticks
Heavens
Mate
There's a roaring primate
Fine
Hen
Zebras gallop to their den.

Joseph McGee (10)
Sandringham Primary School, Doncaster

Food And Sweets

Why do we have food?
To keep the Tyrannosaurus rex in our tummies full.
What are sweets?
Pieces of cheese that went mouldy.
Why can't we drink food?
Because we will die.
Why can't we use food as times tables?
Because teachers are grumpy.

Catrina Stanley (10)
Sandringham Primary School, Doncaster

Weather

What is rain?
When God gets a shower.
What is fog?
When God moves around,
All the dust gets stirred up.
What is thunder?
When God plays His drums.
Where does wind come from?
God farting.
What is snow?
Frozen peas.

Jordan Wykes (11)
Sandringham Primary School, Doncaster

Weather Drums

What is thunder?
God listening to His radio.

What is rain?
God weeing.

What is snow?
Frozen beans.

Where does wind go?
Back to God.

What is fog?
God farting.

Jamie Jones (10)
Sandringham Primary School, Doncaster

Mummy, Why Does It?

'Mummy, why does it thunder?'
'I think it is Heaven and Hell battling.'
'Mummy, why does it rain?'
'Someone is crying.'
'Mummy, why does it hail?'
'It is your dad cleaning out the freezer.'
'Mummy, where does the sun go?'
'The sun goes to sleep like you.'

Gareth Thickett (10)
Sandringham Primary School, Doncaster

Mr Whistle

There is a man from a faraway land,
He held a whistle in his hand,
A mad man made him jump
And he swallowed that whistle in one big lump.

Mr Whistle cannot speak,
He only makes a high-pitched squeak,
He's a good friend you can't prove me wrong,
He whistles all day long.

When he swallowed that whistle,
It made him very ill,
At the time it was quite a thrill,
I'm surprised it wasn't a kill.

Felix Antons-Jones (10)
Sandringham Primary School, Doncaster

Cuddling Daddy

'Daddy, why does our heart beat?'
'Because a man is trapped inside and he is banging to get out.'
'Daddy, why does my tummy rumble when I'm hungry?'
'Because the lion is roaring for food.'
'Daddy, why do I breathe?'
'To let all the goodness enter your body.'
'Daddy, why do I sleep?'
'So the angels can secretly bless you.'
'Goodnight.'

Dorothy Miles (11)
Sandringham Primary School, Doncaster

What Is . . .

What is thunder?
Someone sitting on a cloud smashing cymbals.
What is rain?
God crying.
What are hailstones?
Rabbit droppings from the sky.
Where does the wind go?
To the North Pole.
What is fog?
God dusting Heaven.

Louise Armstrong (10)
Sandringham Primary School, Doncaster

My Mum

My mum has the face of an angel,
Her smile is part of the moon,
Her eyes are like the twinkling stars,
That warm you up at noon!

Harley White (10)
Sandringham Primary School, Doncaster

Sun Shoe

Sun
Shoe
I've made some stew.
Key
Door
It spilt on the floor.
Hive
Mix
I've made some tricks.
Heaven
Date
I've stayed up so late.
Mine
Ben
He ate so much chocolate
He has been sick again.

Charli Holland (10)
Sandringham Primary School, Doncaster

Weather Poem

What is thunder?
I think it is God when He is mad.
Why does it rain?
So plants can grow.
What are hailstones?
When the rain is fast, hailstones come.
Where does the wind go?
It travels all over the world.
What is fog?
It is white air.

Carl Richardson (10)
Sandringham Primary School, Doncaster

Food And Drink

Why do we have to eat food to keep us alive?
So there are enough people in the world.

What is cheese?
Yellow stuff with holes in it.

Why do we have to drink?
Because we need liquid in our body.

What is drink?
Liquid that we drink.

Abigail Thompson (10)
Sandringham Primary School, Doncaster

Weather

What is thunder?
Thunder is God getting mad.
Why does it rain?
It's God having a bath.
What are hailstones?
It's God going to the toilet.
Where does wind go?
To Mars and Pluto.
What is fog?
It's dust from the ground running around.

Chrystal Bissenden (10)
Sandringham Primary School, Doncaster

The Weather Forecast

What is thunder?
God playing His drums.
What is rain?
God crying.
What is snow?
Frozen peas.
Where does wind go?
Back to God.
What is fog?
God burning His food.

Ryan McKenzie (10)
Sandringham Primary School, Doncaster

Pondering Over Computers

If there are CD Roms, and Ram drives, what about sheep?
They might like bus trips
And the mouse!
What about the gerbil
And are loud computers stereotypes?
Why don't keyboards make any noise?
I'm stuck about the web.
I never see any spiders!
Have flat screen computers got run over?
What do computers crash into?
Do they hit hard drives? That would make them flat.
What does the monitor monitor?
Maybe a register.
Would that register with a computer though?
It might not compute with a computer.
All this computer stuff is confusing me. I'll go on the computer . . .

Sam Johnston (9)
Stamford Junior School, Stamford

The Day The Throne Went To Them

When they met the fight began
they got battered and bruised on that day.
Then Richard of the almighty Lancaster
rode to the top of a hill,
he saw Henry standing there alone and bare.
Galloped down and chortled there.
Henry was in sight
but then a Yorkshire man came from behind
and stamped him there.
The spot is marked today
where Richard died on that day.

Louis Grimoldby (10)
Stamford Junior School, Stamford

The Man And The Whale

A man went diving
He saw a blue whale
Trapped in a fishing net
Struggling to stay alive

The men in the fishing boat
They did not care if one little whale died
But this man knew what he should do
So he went to go and help

He set it free with much difficulty
Just as the fishing boat sailed away
The whale swam by, as if saying
'Jump on and I'll take you to the surface', and he did.

Michael Horrell (10)
Stamford Junior School, Stamford

I Have A Big Brother

I have a big brother
And another and another
I call them the thrashing three
Because they always thrash me
They put me to bed
So I can rest my head
But little do they know
What I know
Tonight
I gave them a fright
When I put a rubber spider in their beds!

Alison Murray (10)
Stamford Junior School, Stamford

The Stranger

Once there was a person,
In a long black coat,
Hiding in the shadows,
Watching and waiting.

It saw me stealing money,
It saw me kick the cat,
It saw me breaking windows,
Watching and waiting.

I felt a bit suspicious,
I felt a bit scared,
I felt a bit curious,
To know who was there.

Its waiting time was over,
It revealed itself
To be my head teacher,
Mrs Time herself.

Katie Noble (10)
Stamford Junior School, Stamford

Werewolf

I saw a werewolf,
Phlegm drooping from its fangs,
I try to protect myself
With an embered torch,
Swinging it,
      To and fro,
      To and fro,
But without success.
It was crawling like a lizard,
Trying to provoke me.
I jumped onto my stallion
And rode off into the moonlit night.
      Faster,
      Faster,
Galloped my steed,
I thought I'd lost it . . .
The it pounced and ripped my shoulder,
And now I'm writing this with my enchantment.
Whenever there is a full moon . . .
I will be waiting for you!

Dan Wiggin (10)
Stamford Junior School, Stamford

Tabby Cat

T abby cat, like a furry ball,
A n amazing brown and orange coat.
B y the fire, he purrs and plays
B ut all he needs is love and care
Y et he tries and fails to untangle the wool

C ome and help this soft, sweet bundle,
A ll will be very thankful, just a
T ypical cat wishing to sleep.

Elizabeth Painter (10)
Stamford Junior School, Stamford

Fudge And Toffee

Fudge, fudge, fudge,
Everywhere I see fudge.
The delicious creamy smell
It's just fudge, fudge, fudge
The world is full of fudge,
I think of it every day
But the bit I like is fudge,
Fudge, fudge.

Toffee, toffee, toffee
My heart is full of toffee,
The world I see around me,
Toffee, toffee, toffee,
Toffee is in my brain,
Toffee is in my eyes,
What makes it the best is
Toffee, toffee, toffee.

Thomas Pritchard (11)
Stamford Junior School, Stamford

The Eagle

The Eagle swooped down upon his prey
Talons outstretched; razor sharp
His eyes; little beady, sharp eyes
A smooth coat of feathers
In a flash the small grey mouse
Was clasped in his talons
Blood dribbling from the head
The eagle soared round
Dropped the mouse in his nest
Then flew off to look for more food.

Victoria Salt (10)
Stamford Junior School, Stamford

Elephant

Once there was an elephant
Who lived in a zoo,
I loved the way he ran around
And was the colour blue.

Once there was an elephant
Who went extremely high,
As he looked down
He slipped and started to fly.

Once there was an elephant
Who slept all day,
I thought he had a concussion
But he was faking it all the way.

Once there was an elephant
Which had a bump on his head,
People thought it was cancer,
They were right because he was dead.

Edward Stout (11)
Stamford Junior School, Stamford

Going To School

I'm on my way to school
Rucksack on my back
Blazer on all neat
Books tucked under my arm
Sports bag on my shoulder
Apple in my pocket
A guinea pig up my sleeve
Ain't I so neat, oh yes I am.

Sam Clulow (10)
Stamford Junior School, Stamford

The Dinner Lady

Back to work,
First I've got to make the slurp.
Heat up the ovens and put out the tables and chairs,
Make the gravy, don't forget to take out all the hairs.

That is all you need to know!
Now I'm going to put the toppings on the pizza dough.
They start to come in for a bit of slurp and pizza,
Then more and more come as fast as a cheetah.

Ten minutes later they finally finish saying, 'Bye bye.'
I say, 'Please leave me alone so I can eat my mince pie.'

Fred Forrest (10)
Stamford Junior School, Stamford

The Food Fight

Splat, split, splot
The food fights started now!
Wing, wang, wong
Kids are going wow.

Fing, fang, fong
People are throwing food
Pling, plang, plong
Children are running nude.

Ping, wing, ding
Girls against the boys
Ding, dang, dong
Making such a noise.

Rachel Richardson (10)
Stamford Junior School, Stamford

The Hunter

Once in a jungle
A devil roamed around
It ate food in its path
And was crowned a hunter

No one ever entered
The jungle of doom
In case the king hunter
Attacks with a zoom

So no one ever saw this creature
Because it was a hunter
But a child in the night
Saw two red eyes heading towards him.

Oliver Anand (10)
Stamford Junior School, Stamford

The Rider

Down from the shadows the rider comes,
Down from the land where the supernatural roam.
He taps with his finger on the rusty, hinged door,
Which through its holes moonlight did pour.
The rider stepped in, in his clanking boots
And searched every corner for the eerie loot.
The rider then turned, back to his steed
And galloped away to where the spectral heed.

Jack Lyons (10)
Stamford Junior School, Stamford

Goodbye

Wind blowing through our hair
Leaves swirl, leaving trees bare.

I remember cheerful times
When we fitted as one
Matching like lemons and limes
We always had so much fun.

She arrived from the States
And the words she used were odd
Straight away, we were best mates
Everyone said, 'Two peas in a pod.'

We were different in every way
But that didn't seem to matter
She came to see me every day
Chatter, chatter, chatter.

There was always something we liked to do
Baking gingerbread men with gums and drops
Cakes and brownies and muffins too
And dancing together to Top Of The Pops.

I did her homework and she did mine
I went down to her house nearly all of the time
Now it's all over, our friendship and rhyme
The lemon alone, without the lime.

We've had five fantastic years
With silly giggles and girly cries
Now all our laughs are turning to tears
This is the end, now it's goodbyes.

Wind blowing through my hair
Leaves swirl, leaving trees bare.

Kirsten O'Neill (10)
Stamford Junior School, Stamford

Thy Battle For Middle Earth

Boom! Goes thy horn of thee Urak-hai,
Thy brave five cultures are willing to die,
These soldiers freezing in their walls of rock,
As thy Orcs pull up to thy derelict dock.

Thy Orcs are hoping for a bloodshed war,
Shields are going to be shattered for sure,
Thy Elves can feel thy mournful night,
As thy soldiers dread thy terrible sight.

As they step unto thy enemies' lair,
Thy fear of evil thickens thy air.
See thy reverence and determination in thy soldiers' faces,
Within thy forms and sizes and races.

Gimli; very deceiving of his height,
Proves himself a good fighter with pure, sturdy might.
An excellent character, but fierce with his axe,
He can follow and defeat enemies in their tracks!

As thy furious battle has begun,
Many sacrificing their lives for evil's curse to be undone,
Legolas; thy Elvin king, a born fighter at war,
Shivers as he hears thy Urak-hai *roar!*

A great battle is commencing; win, they must,
Yet still thy fellowship needs faith and trust.
Orcs fall to thy floor as a shower of arrows drop,
Urak-hai lift their ladders to climb up to thy top,
Saruman's army, outnumbering them,
Fall to their doom with thy large sword's stem,

Thy battle is won and Sauron is defeated,
Thy mission to save Middle Earth has now been completed,
Now Aragorn, at last, has become king,
Thy fellowship have great gifts to bring.

Amardeep Singh Bhaker (10)
Stamford Junior School, Stamford

The Mystery Person

I'm sure I saw it Mum, I really, really am!
It could have carved me into a thick piece of ham
Don't make me go back there again
I'll plead with you till I die
Please don't let him put me in a baked apple pie.

I'm sure I saw it Mum, I really, really am!
Its horse is a deep, deep black,
It looks like it's been friends with my old cousin Jack
Please can you believe me
Or else I'll jump in the sea.

I'm sure I saw it Mum, I really, really am!
I think he was a man,
'Well what was his name then?'
His name was Dad
But I think he was turning really, really mad.

Justin Bland (10)
Stamford Junior School, Stamford

Funny Friday

Today I'm going riding,
But my pony's hiding,
I can't find him,
His coat colour is dim,
So I can't see him easily,

I am in town,
I see a flash of dark brown,
I think that was my pony,
So now I have to catch him,
This is not going to be easy.

Elinor Lloyd (10)
Stamford Junior School, Stamford

Gymnastics

G irls and boys doing gymnastics
Y oung children working hard
M en and women competing in competitions
N asty accidents can happen
A chieving targets
S howing determination
T umbling, vaulting, all sorts of stuff
I nteresting routines
C oaches doing their best to teach the gymnasts
S howing enthusiasm, achieving things and having fun,
   that's what gymnastics is about.

Angelina Radjenovic (10)
Stamford Junior School, Stamford

Kingfisher Song

K ingfisher, kingfisher,
I n a plum tree,
N ever thought to look at me,
G ently gazing down at a stream,
F ish, fish, everywhere,
I like to see them all,
S wimming in the current,
H urry, swoop down kingfisher,
E ating them greedily and,
R acing far away.

S inging with happiness,
O nly him and me around,
N ot knowing I was there,
G littering in the pearly mist.

Emily Rowbotham (10)
Stamford Junior School, Stamford

My Family

My mum is ill
she needs her pill,
I lost the pill
so she stays ill.

My dad is sad
he wants his lad,
his lad's being bad
so he stays sad.

My brother's gone
to sing a song,
I went along
and sang the song.

I am in bed
I've cracked my head,
my dad had said
to stay in bed.

My granny's out
she said about,
my grandad's snout
has to come out!

My cousin's cool
but he likes school,
I think he's tall
he is so cool!

Alice Reid (10)
Stamford Junior School, Stamford

A Golden Eagle

As the golden eagle,
Swoops high and low,
Searching for its prey,
Wondering where to look for grub,
Because nowhere is there food in sight.

The golden bird,
Sways left and right,
His big beady eyes
And his beak as sharp as a sword,
Searching for thy fine chow.

Getting further and further away,
From his home and his life,
Getting more worried as he is only a baby,
Suddenly shots rang out,
With a smell of fierce hunters.

Flying its little heart out,
With almost no energy left,
Getting slower and slower then,
Out of nowhere a bird that is unknown,
Swooped down to save him
But the bird was shot!

Even though the bird is dead,
It did save the eagle's life,
Because the hunters left,
Pleased with what they had shot,
The bird got home and lived his life.

The golden eagle is now grown up,
With children that have just been born,
Living a happy life in a place that is free
Teaching his toddlers how to fly,
Ready to live alone.

Jamie Ridgeon (10)
Stamford Junior School, Stamford

Where A Baby Elephant Stood

I went to the circus,
To watch the clowns and seals,
But when I sat down,
I wished this wasn't real.

For a baby elephant stood,
On the platforms high,
And now I knew,
That this elephant was shy.

And as I looked closer,
A tear fell from his eye,
Now I knew,
That he was going to cry.

Suddenly the tamer whipped his leg
And somehow he gave me a clue
That he wanted to be in Africa
With the other elephants too.

James Wilde (11)
Stamford Junior School, Stamford

Morris The Monkey

There was a monkey called Morris
Morris lived in a bowl
Morris swung from tree to tree
Morris meets monkeys every day
Morris lived in a bowl

Morris met a monkey one day
Morris his name was
Morris and Morris were brothers
They still lived in a bowl.

Izaac Grimoldby (10)
Stamford Junior School, Stamford

A Scary Hairy Safari Trip

A scary, hairy safari trip,
Soggy, boggy, try not to slip,
Swishy, swashy, duck your head,
Creepy-crawlies on my blood have fed.

Snarls, growls, what is there?
Yelps and howls must beware,
Screeches, squeals don't be a baby,
We are safe with our guide, well maybe?

Hissing, crackling, warming fire,
Our situation is getting dire.
Delicious meaty dinner smells,
The animals want to join in as well.

Shiny teeth like stars appear,
Shaky knees wobble with fear,
Rustling, bustling in the trees,
Won't someone come and rescue me please!

Chloë Powell (10)
Stamford Junior School, Stamford

My Puppy

Tail wagger
Bone chewer
Ball chaser
Walk lover
Food taker
Friend maker
Lead tugger
Home racer
House wrecker
Space user
River swimming
Sun bather.

Florence Thompson (10)
Stamford Junior School, Stamford

On The Way To The Mine

On the way to the mine
I saw a dark, dingy dungeon,
Upon it stood the head of a lion,
It was full of rock solid iron.

I went in cautiously,
The cackles of witches,
The laugh of men,
The cries of slaves.

I gripped my pick axe,
Ready for the blow,
I hear metal clash,
I feel my blood flow.

Josh Riddick (10)
Stamford Junior School, Stamford

My Night Out

Splish, splash, splosh
The gravy's looking green.
Whoosh, smoosh, moosh,
Mash potato hit the queen.

Whack, crack, thwack
I think it has only started.
Bang, tang, mang
It's time that we departed.

Crash, smash, bash
The waitress is in shock.
Thunk, bunk, dunk,
Custard tart is on her frock.

Anna Roe (10)
Stamford Junior School, Stamford

The Furry Thing

I was sitting at my table doing some maths
Then I saw a furry, fuzzy thing taking a bath
It was on my teacher's desk looking through his stuff
                                    with such interest
It looked at me and shrieked at me, *ssh!* and crawled up his vest
First I thought I was seeing things so I rubbed my eyes to check
I opened my eyes to see what he was hiding round his neck
I went to tell the teacher but he would have thought I'd gone mad
So I just got on with my work but couldn't because I felt so bad.

Alexia Thorne (11)
Stamford Junior School, Stamford

Haunted House

I went to a haunted house one day,
To see what I could do, and play.
I saw a shadow, it spooked me out,
So now I'm scared, so let me out!

All of a sudden a skeleton appeared,
Now I'm shaking, this is really weird.
I need some help to find my way back,
But with no one around, how could I do that?

As I wondered mindlessly,
I thought my mum would be missing me.
Then I saw a red-eyed cat,
Pouncing on a beastly bat.

'It's a dream, it's a dream!' I said to myself,
Then I saw a phone on the shelf.
I picked it up and tried to phone,
'Please oh please pick me up at home.'

Gabrielle Bangay (10)
Stamford Junior School, Stamford

The Pet Shop

When I grow up
I would like to own a pet shop,
with puppies, kittens and goldfish alike,
hamsters, gerbils, rabbits and mice
and perhaps a chinchilla
would also be nice.

Or maybe a python,
that would crush you to death,
with shiny green scales,
and venomy breath,
budgies, canaries,
a mean-looking rat,
or a beautiful, well-groomed
white Persian cat!

I'd have tropical fish,
from a warm, foreign sea,
guinea pigs, ferrets,
every pet there could be,
every pet in the world, would
be there in my shop,
once I get going,
I can't seem to stop!

Fleurie Crozier (10)
Stamford Junior School, Stamford

My Favourite Colour

My favourite colour is bright
My favourite colour is light
My favourite colour could be anything but blue

My favourite colour is in my room
My favourite colour is blossom that blooms
My favourite colour is . . . *pink!*

Chloe Stowers-Veitch (10)
Stamford Junior School, Stamford

Challenge Me If You Dare

The black shadow rides on,
He passes the carriage,
He has no choice but to stop,
Well he wants to stop,
'Stand and deliver,
Challenge me if you dare.'

Brave as a lion,
Cunning as a fox,
Sleek as a cat,
He will not take off his lucky hat,
'Stand and deliver,
Challenge me if you dare.'

Do not stroll into the woods
Unless you want to feel the shadow's lead,
He will rip, he will tear,
He will spread your pieces everywhere.
'Stand and deliver,
Challenge me if you dare?'

Douglas Tawn (10)
Stamford Junior School, Stamford

Chocolate

I love chocolate,
It melts in my mouth,
It makes me want to live down in the south.
I love chocolate,
I love every single kind,
My mouth starts to water, it blows me out of my mind.
I love chocolate,
You find it all over my house,
Everybody loves chocolate even my pet mouse.

Hebe Fox (10)
Stamford Junior School, Stamford

Racoons

'Get out,' I bark. 'Get out.'
The racoons tipped the table over.
'Argh,' I yell. 'Argh.'
Now they've got in the Land Rover.

'No,' I drone. 'No,
Not the special china,
Please,' I cry. 'Please.'
The damage is not minor.

'Not my house,' I scream. 'Not my house.'
The curtains have lots of tears.
'I beg you,' I shout. 'I beg you
Please go down the stairs.'

'Go away,' I shout. 'Go away,
Go out and play.'
'Hurray,' I cry. 'Hurray.'
Now they've gone away.

Victoria Burgess (10)
Stamford Junior School, Stamford

What Am I?

I am as slow as a snail
But I swing through the tree tops.
I have fur and I have eighteen hours sleep,
What could I be?

I have claws on my hand and feet,
I am lazy and as thick as a sheep.
You can find monkeys where I live,
What could I be?

I am a sloth.

Guy Sinker (10)
Stamford Junior School, Stamford

The Jungle

Insects crawling up the trees,
Dark, scary, *ahh* there's bees,
Bushes shaking,
Loud noise they're making.

Birds squawking fly away,
Lions roaming all day,
Monkey jumping
From tree to tree.

That's all I've got to say,
So have a nice day.

Ella Grimoldby (10)
Stamford Junior School, Stamford

Fantastic School

Croc in the kitchen,
Food fight in the hall,
Glass in the corridor,
Teachers watching all.

Tiger in the changing room,
Otters in the pool,
Skateboards in the classroom,
Rebellious children rule.

Tarantula in the library,
Scorpions on teachers' heads,
Bikes in the gym hall,
Slugs in boarders' beds.

Wow what a fantastic school!

Alexander Griffin (10)
Stamford Junior School, Stamford

Dustbin Monster

I am the dustbin monster,
I live outside a house,
Scaring off the stray cats
And frightening Sarah's mouse.
I love to live in rubbish,
Rubbish is my life.

Rubbish is delightful, rubbish is lush,
Living in free food all day.
I love to live in rubbish, although that's just me,
Now I think it's time for tea,
I need to find my old turkey so leave me be.

George Pears (10)
Stamford Junior School, Stamford

After School

After school my brother and I always have a race
And when I win you should see the look on his face.

The bell rings,
Everybody rushes out,
My brother and I race to the sweet shop.

My head is always the commentator,
And Tim is in the lead,
Alex has got the money though so it's a tie.
Oh and look at that, Tim has tripped Alex up,
What's that? Tim has got the money,
There's all to play for now.

We both sprint to the sweet shop,
I have the money,
Let's see there's Hubba Bubba, Skittles, Maltesers. . .
Oh yeah! I can buy all of them!
My brother says, 'You're disqualified!'
I will leave the rest to your imagination . . .

Catherine Terry (10)
Stamford Junior School, Stamford

My Little Sister

My little baby sister
Is a right pain,
She steals all my toys,
I never see them again.

When *she* kicks *me*
I always get the blame,
Even when Mum sees,
I don't get the game.

It's like a war,
Three against one,
Mum gets crazy all the time,
She's even worse than Don.

She makes me mad all over,
Don does too.
But the worst time is
When she thinks my bedroom is the loo!

But she's trying to be affectionate,
That I can see,
But she does make me mental
When she buzzes like a bee.

She is my little sister,
Now I can see
And as some people say,
I love thee.

Holly Archer (10)
Stamford Junior School, Stamford

Pink Shoes

Walking down the corridor,
Walking down the street,
Hoping no one notices
The things upon my feet!

Oh no it can't be,
I can feel my face going red,
It's my worst enemy,
Big bullying Ted.

And suddenly he shouted,
For the whole street to hear,
'You've got pink shoes on,'
As the street started to sneer,

I took off my shoes,
And threw them in a lake,
Thinking of those people,
What a fuss to make.

When I got home,
Barefooted, tired and red,
My mum gave me some cocoa
And tucked me into bed!

Simon Taylor (10)
Stamford Junior School, Stamford

Graveyard Gloom

As the clock strikes midnight
I run, I run
As I wander through the graveyard,
This surely isn't fun.

The living dead arises
And I am their prey tonight.
They smell my flesh and smile
So I run with all my might.

They gather in a circle,
Their breath as cold as ice.
My face is covered in sweat,
It's creepier than mice.

With ragged cloaks, they glide
Towards me, I feel bad.
Then they all cackle loudly,
It's like they've all gone mad.

As the clock strikes midnight
I run, I run
As I wander through the graveyard
This surely isn't fun
And then I woke up.

Nikki Bows (10)
Stamford Junior School, Stamford

Food Fight

It all started with chocolate cake,
A small piece thrown by mistake,
A boy then spilt his chicken soup
And the teams started to group.

Us versus them at 12.05,
All with ammo; cheese and pork pies,
The battle commenced - food was thrown in the air,
The poor old chef thought it was too much to bear.

Gloop, glump went the chocolate mousse,
Drip-drop went the orange juice,
Duck, carrots and roast potatoes
All hitting people on these tables to those.

Screaming and laughter and howling and mourning,
Then from above, salad dressing came falling,
The commotion died down, and everyone took cover,
Some under tables and some in the oven.

For ten minutes we sheltered,
Until the dressing had melted,
We cautiously climbed out of our hiding protection,
Together we gazed at the waxed floor in affection.

We slid and we skidded, on the dressing covered floor,
When all of a sudden a figure burst through the door,
We stared around at our unbelievable feature
And then at the quivering silhouette of our head teacher.

Before she could burst and go puce in the face,
Something stopped her dead, rooted in place,
A half-eaten doughnut thrown by a 4th year,
Punched into her stomach, forcing her onto her rear.

Joe Cameron (10)
Stamford Junior School, Stamford